WASHINGTON
COMMANDERS

BY JOSH ANDERSON

Stride

An Imprint of The Child's World®
childsworld.com

The Child's World®
childsworld.com

Published by The Child's World®
800-599-READ • www.childsworld.com

Photography Credits
Cover: © Christian Petersen / Staff / Getty Images; page 1: © Africa Studio / Shutterstock; page 3: © Patrick Smith / Staff / Getty Images; page 5: © Patrick Smith / Staff / Getty Images; page 6: © Staff / Getty Images; page 9: © Dustin Satloff / Stringer / Getty Images; page 10: © Rob Carr / Staff / Getty Images; page 11: © stevezmina1 / Getty Images; page 12: © Todd Olszewski / Stringer / Getty Images; page 12: © Mitchell Leff / Stringer / Getty Images; page 13: © Everett Collection / Newscom; page 13: © Mitchell Layton / Stringer / Getty Images; page 14: © Rob Carr / Staff / Getty Images; page 15: © Christian Petersen / Staff / Getty Images; page 16: © Everett Collection / Newscom; page 16: © David Durochik / Associated Press; page 17: © John McDonough/Icon SMI / Newscom; page 17: © Scott Cunningham / Stringer / Getty Images; page 18: © JT Vintage/ZUMA Press / Newscom; page 18: © Arnie Sachs/ZUMA Press / Newscom; page 19: © Staff / Getty Images; page 19: © Mike Powell / Staff / Getty Images; page 20: © Rey Del Rio / Stringer / Getty Images; page 20: © Patrick Smith / Staff / Getty Images; page 21: © Scott Taetsch / Stringer / Getty Images; page 21: © Greg Fiume / Stringer / Getty Images; page 22: © Jamie Squire / Staff / Getty Images; page 23: © Rick Stewart / Stringer / Getty Images; page 23: © stevezmina1 / Getty Images; page 25: © Jonathan Daniel / Stringer / Getty Images; page 26: © Brian Killian / Stringer / Getty Images; page 29: © George Rose / Stringer / Getty Images

ISBN Information
9781503857841 (Reinforced Library Binding)
9781503860698 (Portable Document Format)
9781503862050 (Online Multi-user eBook)
9781503863415 (Electronic Publication)

LCCN 2021952683

Printed in the United States of America

TABLE OF CONTENTS

GO COMMANDERS!

The Washington Commanders compete in the National Football **League's** (NFL's) National Football Conference (NFC). They play in the NFC East **division**, along with the Dallas Cowboys, New York Giants, and Philadelphia Eagles. The rivalries in the NFC East are some of the oldest and fiercest in the entire NFL. Washington has won three **Super Bowls** in their history, all within a ten-year period between 1982 and 1991. Let's learn more about the Washington Commanders!

NFC EAST DIVISION

Dallas Cowboys

New York Giants

Philadelphia Eagles

Washington Commanders

WASHINGTON MADE IT BACK TO THE PLAYOFFS IN 2020 FOR THE FIRST TIME IN FIVE SEASONS.

BECOMING THE COMMANDERS

The Commanders began play in 1932 in Boston, Massachusetts. They were called the Boston Braves. A year later, the team changed its name to the Boston Redskins. In 1937, the team moved to Washington, D.C., where they played until 1996. In 1997, the team moved into a new **stadium**, FedEx Field, located 11 miles (18 km) from Washington, D.C., in North Englewood, Maryland. Because the team's name was considered by many to be offensive to Native Americans, the team was temporarily called the Washington Football Team from 2020 through the end of the 2021 season. They officially became the Washington Commanders ahead of the 2022 season.

WASHINGTON WAS ONE OF THE DOMINANT TEAMS IN THE NFL DURING THE 1980S AND EARLY 1990S.

BY THE NUMBERS

The Washington Commanders have won **THREE** Super Bowls.

16 division titles for the team

541 points scored by the Commanders in 1983—a team record!

14 wins for the team in 1991

RUNNING BACK ANTONIO GIBSON GAINED 1,832 RUSHING YARDS IN HIS FIRST TWO SEASONS WITH THE TEAM.

WASHINGTON HAS MADE THE PLAYOFFS SIX TIMES SINCE MOVING INTO FEDEX FIELD IN 1997.

The Washington Commanders have had three home stadiums since moving from Boston to the nation's capital. They played in Griffith Stadium, which they shared with the Washington Senators baseball team, from 1937 to 1960. Then they played in Robert F. Kennedy Memorial Stadium from 1961 to 1996. Since 1997, the team's home has been FedEx Field. On game days, FedEx Field holds 82,000 Washington fans. On January 8, 2000, the Washington Commanders won the first-ever **playoff** game at FedEx Field, defeating the Detroit Lions 27–13.

We're Famous!

One of the National Basketball Association's (NBA) top players may also be the Washington Commanders' biggest fan. NBA star Kevin Durant of the Brooklyn Nets grew up in Maryland, five minutes from FedEx Field. As a kid, he became a huge fan and even has a tattoo of the team logo on his arm. Durant has said he wants to own an NFL team when he retires. He said his first option would be to try to buy his hometown squad!

UNIFORM

MAROON

WHITE

Truly Weird

Washington finished the 1940 NFL season with a 9–2 record. That was the best in the entire league that season. But it didn't help them at all in the NFL Championship Game against the 8–3 Chicago Bears. The Bears intercepted eight passes and won the game 73–0. That's the largest victory margin in NFL history!

Alternate Jersey

Sometimes teams wear an alternate jersey that is different from their home and away jerseys. It might be a bright color or have a unique theme. For a 2020 game against the Cincinnati Bengals, Washington wore old "throwback" uniforms with maroon and tan colors similar to what the team wore early in their history. The new look proved lucky. Washington won the game.

LOYAL FANS ARE ALWAYS EAGER TO CONGRATULATE THEIR FAVORITE PLAYERS ON A WIN AT FEDEX FIELD.

Fans waited eagerly throughout the 2020 and 2021 seasons to find out what new name would be chosen for Washington's football team. In 2021, a team executive revealed some of the names being considered for the team. Some options were "Red Hogs," "Defenders," "Armada," "Presidents," and "Brigade." In the end, the team was named the "Commanders." Also in 2021, the team added an element to the game experience for fans. The Washington Football Team's co-ed dance team now entertains fans at every home game and at other local community events too.

HEROES OF HISTORY

Sammy Baugh
Quarterback/Defensive Back | 1937–1952

Baugh was one of the brightest stars of the NFL during the 1930s and 1940s. He led the league in completion percentage eight times and passing yards four times. In the era before the Super Bowl, he led Washington to the NFL Championship twice. He is a member of the Pro Football **Hall of Fame**.

Chris Hanburger
Linebacker | 1965–1978

Hanburger was a dominant defensive force for Washington in the 1960s and 1970s. He helped lead the team to Super Bowl 7 after the 1972 season. He finished his career with 19 interceptions. Hanburger was chosen for nine **Pro Bowls**. In 2011, he was inducted into the Pro Football Hall of Fame.

Art Monk
Wide Receiver | 1980–1993

Monk was a key contributor on three Washington teams that won the Super Bowl. During his 14 seasons in Washington, Monk totaled more than 1,000 receiving yards five times. He led the league with 106 receptions in 1984. Monk was chosen for three Pro Bowls. He's a member of the Pro Football Hall of Fame.

Joe Theismann
Quarterback | 1974–1985

Theismann led Washington to victory in Super Bowl 17 after the 1982 NFL season. In 1983, Theismann finished with 29 **touchdown** passes and only 11 interceptions. That year, he was named the NFL's **Most Valuable Player** (MVP). Theismann finished his career with a 77–47 record as Washington's starting quarterback. He was chosen for the Pro Bowl twice.

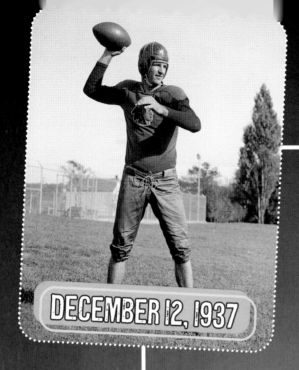

Washington defeats the Chicago Bears 28–21 in the NFL Championship Game.

DECEMBER 12, 1937

The team advances to its first Super Bowl by defeating the Dallas Cowboys 26–3 in the NFC Championship Game.

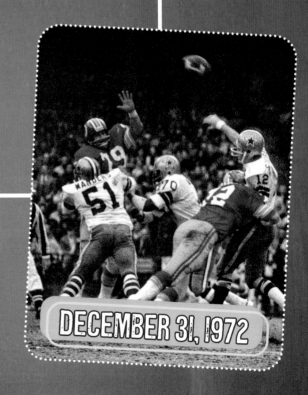

DECEMBER 31, 1972

BIG DAYS

JANUARY 30, 1983

Washington wins the first Super Bowl in its history, beating the Miami Dolphins 27–17.

In Super Bowl 22, Washington earns a decisive victory over the Denver Broncos, 42–10.

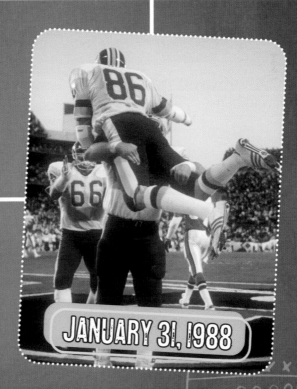

JANUARY 31, 1988

MODERN-DAY MARVELS

Antonio Gibson
Running Back | Debut: 2020

Washington chose Gibson with a third-round pick in the 2020 NFL Draft. As a **rookie**, Gibson rushed for 795 yards. He also finished with 11 rushing touchdowns. In 2020, Gibson became the first rookie in more than 20 years to score three touchdowns on Thanksgiving Day. He rushed for 1,037 yards in 2021 and scored ten touchdowns.

Terry McLaurin
Wide Receiver | Debut: 2019

After he starred at Ohio State University, Washington picked McLaurin in the third round of the 2019 NFL Draft. He led Washington in receiving during each of his first three seasons. He achieved his first season with more than 1,000 yards in 2020. In his first-ever playoff game, McLaurin caught six passes for 75 receiving yards.

Carson Wentz
Quarterback | Debut: 2022

Wentz began his career with the Philadelphia Eagles. After playing one season with the Indianapolis Colts in 2021, Wentz was traded to the Commanders. In his first six seasons, Wentz won 44 games as a starting quarterback. He was selected for the Pro Bowl after the 2017 season.

Chase Young
Defensive End | Debut: 2020

Young dominated college football during his final season at Ohio State University. Washington then picked him second overall in the 2020 NFL Draft. As a rookie, Young finished with four forced fumbles and 7.5 **sacks**. He was selected for the Pro Bowl and picked as the NFL's Defensive Rookie of the Year.

OVER TWO DECADES, CORNERBACK DARRELL GREEN ESTABLISHED HIMSELF AS THE GREATEST WASHINGTON FOOTBALL PLAYER OF THEM ALL.

DARRELL GREEN

Considered one of the fastest players ever to compete in the NFL, Green was nicknamed the "Ageless Wonder." The nickname fit because Green played at a high level for 20 seasons, until he retired at 42 years old. He ranks 21st all-time with 54 career interceptions. Green led Washington to two Super Bowl titles. He was chosen for the Pro Bowl seven times and is a member of the Pro Football Hall of Fame.

FAN FAVORITE

Mark Rypien–Quarterback
1988–1993

Rypien will be forever loved by fans for his success in 1991. That year, he led the team to a 14–2 record in the regular season and victory in Super Bowl 26. Overall, Rypien led the team to 45 wins over six seasons. He was chosen for the Pro Bowl twice.

#1

THE BIG GAME

Washington's appearance in Super Bowl 26 was the team's third trip to the big game in ten years. Their opponent was the Buffalo Bills. Any doubt about the game's outcome had been settled by early in the third quarter when Washington took a 24–0 lead on a two-yard rush by Gerald Riggs. After throwing for 292 yards and two touchdowns, Washington quarterback Mark Rypien was named the game's MVP. After winning their third Super Bowl in a decade, Washington would not get a chance to play in the big game at all over the next 30 seasons.

WIDE RECEIVER GARY CLARK HAD
114 RECEIVING YARDS AND CAUGHT A
TOUCHDOWN IN SUPER BOWL 26.

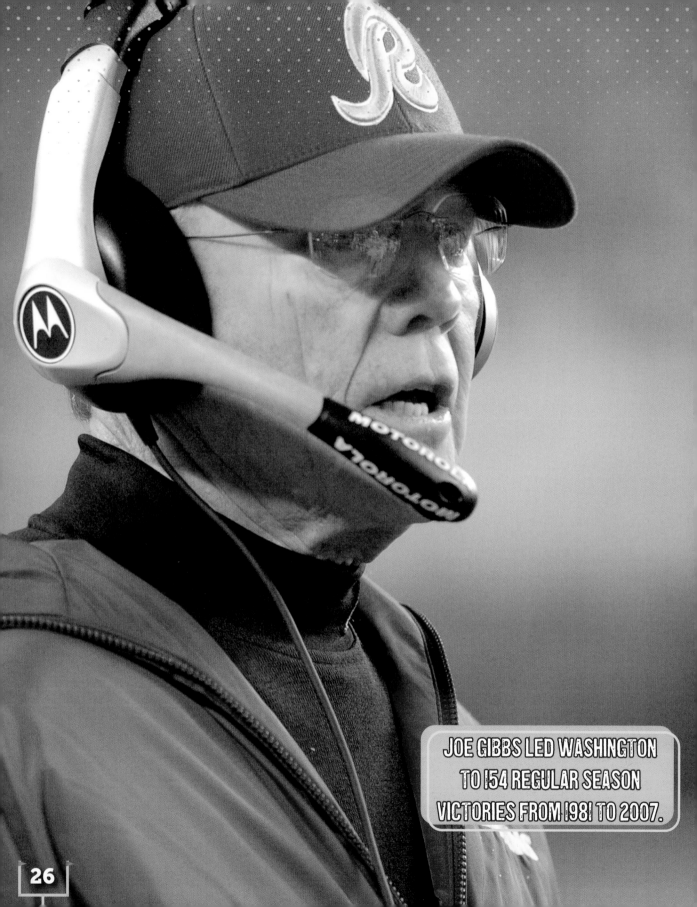

JOE GIBBS LED WASHINGTON TO 154 REGULAR SEASON VICTORIES FROM 1981 TO 2007.

AMAZING FEATS

1,483 Passing Yards

In 2016 by **QUARTERBACK** Kirk Cousins

31 Passing Touchdowns

In 1967 by **QUARTERBACK** Sonny Jurgensen

24 Rushing Touchdowns

In 1983 for **RUNNING BACK** John Riggins

4,917 Receiving Yards

In 2005 for **WIDE RECEIVER** Santana Moss

ALL-TIME BEST

PASSING YARDS

Joe Theismann
25,206

Sonny Jurgensen
22,585

Sammy Baugh
21,886

RUSHING YARDS

John Riggins
7,472

Clinton Portis
6,824

Larry Brown
5,875

RECEIVING YARDS

Art Monk
12,026

Charley Taylor
9,110

Gary Clark
8,742

SACKS*

Dexter Manley
97

Ryan Kerrigan
95.5

Charles Mann
82

SCORING

Mark Moseley
1,206

Chip Lohmiller
787

Dustin Hopkins
668

INTERCEPTIONS

Darrell Green
54

Brig Owens
36

Sammy Baugh
31

*unofficial before 1982

IT OFTEN TOOK A WHOLE GROUP OF TACKLERS TO BRING DOWN WASHINGTON'S ALL-TIME LEADING RUSHER JOHN RIGGINS.

GLOSSARY

division (dih-VIZSH-un): a group of teams within the NFL that play each other more frequently and compete for the best record

Hall of Fame (HAHL of FAYM): a museum in Canton, Ohio, that honors the best players in NFL history

league (LEEG): an organization of sports teams that compete against each other

Most Valuable Player (MOHST VAL-yuh-bul PLAY-uhr): a yearly award given to the top player in the NFL

playoffs (PLAY-ahfs): a series of games after the regular season that decides which two teams play in the Super Bowl

Pro Bowl (PRO BOWL): the NFL's All-Star game where the best players in the league compete

rookie (RUH-kee): a player playing in his first season

sack (SAK): when a quarterback is tackled behind the line of scrimmage before he can throw the ball

stadium (STAY-dee-um): a building with a field and seats for fans where teams play

Super Bowl (SOO-puhr BOWL): the championship game of the NFL, played between the winners of the AFC and the NFC

touchdown (TUTCH-down): a play in which the ball is brought into the other team's end zone, resulting in six points

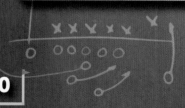

IN THE LIBRARY

Bulgar, Beth and Mark Bechtel. *My First Book of Football.*
New York, NY: Time Inc. Books, 2015.

Jacobs, Greg. *The Everything Kids' Football Book, 7th Edition*.
Avon, MA: Adams Media, 2021.

Sports Illustrated Kids. *The Greatest Football Teams of All Time*.
New York, NY: Time Inc. Books, 2018.

Temple, Ramey. *Washington Redskins*. New York, NY: AV2 Books, 2020.

ON THE WEB

Visit our website for links about the Washington Commanders:
childsworld.com/links

Note to parents, teachers, and librarians: We routinely verify our web links to make sure they are safe and active sites. Encourage your readers to check them out!

ABOUT THE AUTHOR

Josh Anderson has published over 50 books for children and young adults. His two boys are the greatest joys in his life. Hobbies include coaching his sons in youth basketball, no-holds-barred games of Apples to Apples, and taking long family walks. His favorite NFL team is a secret he'll never share!